TOKYOPOP 2003
SNEAK PEEK SAMPLER

TOKYOPOP
LOS ANGELES · TOKYO · LONDON

TOKYOPOP 2003
SNEAK PEEK SAMPLER

Left to Right >>>

Table of Contents

Introduction

Congratulations on getting your hands on the
ultra-exclusive TOKYOPOP 2003 Manga Sampler! As a
sophisticated reader, you might notice that there's
something different about this book. This manga
sampler not only includes the 100% authentic format, but also includes a section containing manga
in the left-to-right format that showcases works
by American and Korean manga artists! Now, you get
the best of both worlds!

TOKYOPOP, founded in 1996, is the leading North
American publisher of manga, the fastest-growing
category within the publishing business. With
exclusive rights to hundreds of book, video and
music properties, the company has become a media
convergence leader. TOKYOPOP has millions of
books in print and publishes several hit properties
based on popular Cartoon Network and Kids! WB
programs. TOKYOPOP titles include *Sailor Moon,
Gundam, Initial D, Samurai Girl: Real Bout High
School, Reign: The Conqueror* and *Cowboy Bebop,*
among others. With rapidly growing U.S. demand for
its properties, TOKYOPOP is actively expanding
into television, film and licensed goods. Visit
www.TOKYOPOP.com for additional information.

DEMON DIARY

Introduction:

Meet Raenef—a newly appointed
demon lord who doesn't quite know
what he's doing—and his teacher,
Eclipse—a wise and noble demon
who's been given the daunting job of
whipping Raenef into a proper demon
lord. At first, Eclipse finds
Raenef's meek, cheerful and kind-
hearted nature annoyingly unbefit-
ting of a demon lord. The more time
they spend together, the more
Eclipse finds himself strangely
drawn to Raenef. Join these two (and
the knights, priests, gods and demons
they meet along the way) on their
journey of friendship and discovery.

Demon Diary was created by Kara,
one of the top shonen-ai artists in
Korea.

Created by:

Lee Chi Hyong
Kara

Release Date:

Vol. 01   05/06/03
Vol. 02   07/08/03
Vol. 03   09/09/03
Vol. 04   11/04/04

T
TEEN
AGE 13+

...a demon lord?

DEMON DIARY

마왕일기

그림 / 카라   글 / 이지형

Hey, I took this job for the free food and housing, but...

...I'm not exactly sure what I've signed up for.

You've heard tales of ancient knights, have you not?

Yessir

You need only emulate the demon lords of lore.

Of lore?

I should set fires, wreak havoc and conspire to take over the world?

I will kill you, vile demon!

Mooahahaha! Die, Fool!

Boo hoo hoo! Save me, gallant knight!

Oh! Maybe kidnap a princess and get trounced by a knight!

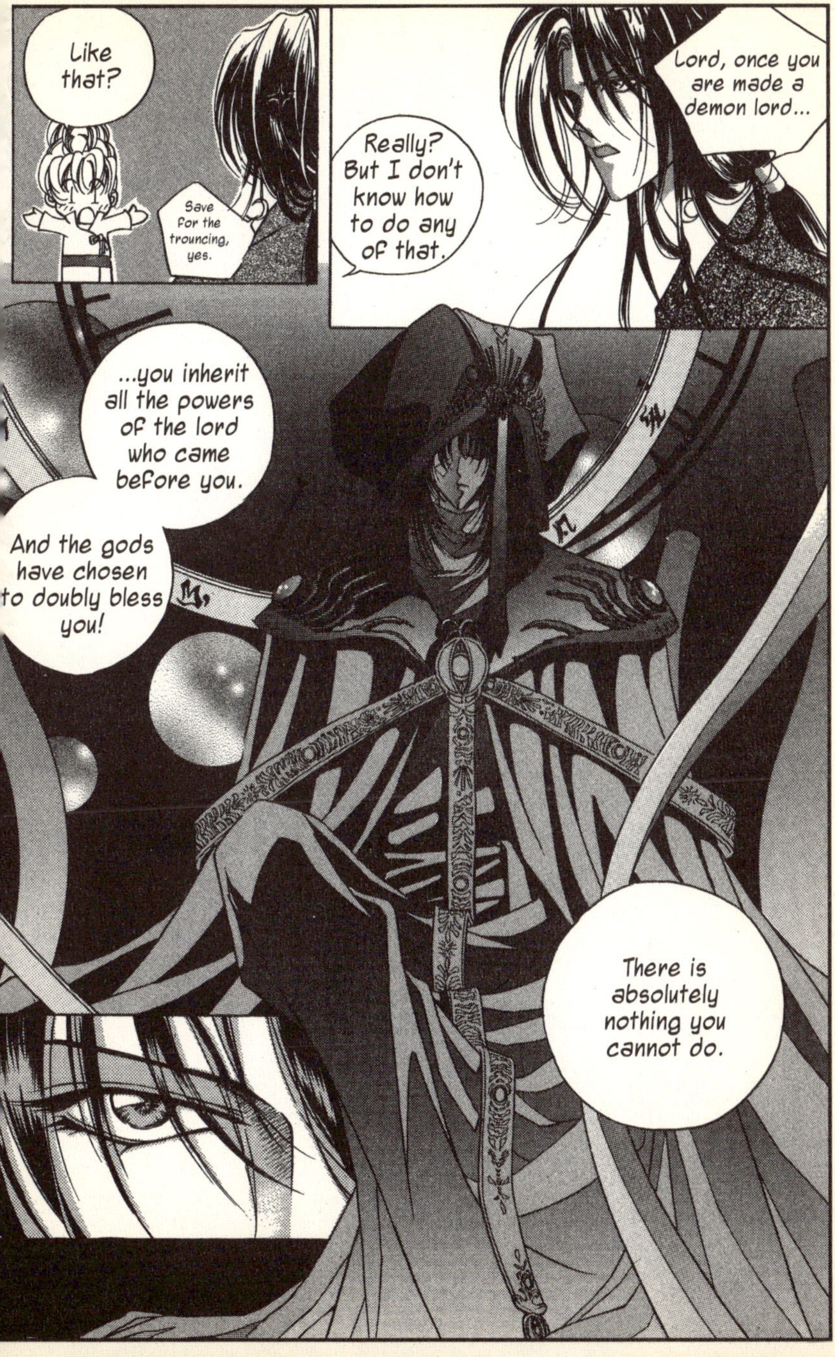

Like that?
Save for the trouncing, yes.
Really? But I don't know how to do any of that.
Lord, once you are made a demon lord...
...you inherit all the powers of the lord who came before you.
And the gods have chosen to doubly bless you!
There is absolutely nothing you cannot do.

I'm doubly blessed, mister?

......

You'll be fine.

Now, I must ask you not to address me as "sir" or "mister."

How come?

A demon lord does not defer A demon lord instills terror and exudes superiority.

I don't want to terrorize any-body, mister.

YOU WILL REIGN IN TERROR WHETHER YOU LIKE IT OR NOT!

To do otherwise would make a laughingstock of us both.

Well, exCUSE me, mist--

I mean--ulp-- sorry...fella.

A demon lord never apologizes, either. No matter what.

Why not...?

I have a funny feeling about this one...

.....

I suppose that's better, but...

He's quite unlike his predecessor.

Because a demon lord must appear wicked.

How can I make this clear?

Do you understand?

Ahem.

In an instance such as that of a moment ago, rather than apologize...

Yep. Piece of cake.

...it would be appropriate to adopt a haughty tone and ask, "How dare YOU admonish ME, vermin?"

I suppose I don't know him well enough...yet.

This does not bode well.

11

All right, just lease hurry and get ready. I'll wait for you here.

All right-- I did it!

Okay--how do I get to my room again?

For the LAST TIME--

Sorry...

Wherever you want to go within this castle, you need only picture it in your mind and say "go."

Pi! .How dare YOU admonish ME... vermin?

Pi! Pi!

......

Oh, this...this is going to be a long and difficult road...

I better split before Demon Grumpmeister goes ballistic.

Go!

I.N.V.U.

Introduction:

Sey Hong is a skittish teenage girl whose mom has left her in the care of an old friend. Now living in what appears to be the perfect family, Sey finds out that Terry—apparently the son of the house—is really Hali, the daughter. Terry died in an accident but his mom could not accept it. Hali was forced to impersonate Terry to keep her mom from suffering a mental breakdown. Things continue to get more complicated as Sey finds out that Hali is in love with the same male teacher that Sey has had a crush on for years. And those are just a few of the twists in this gender-bending new shojo series from TOKYOPOP!

Created by:
Kim Kang Won

Release Date:

T
TEEN
AGE 13+

YOU LIVE IN ONE OF THE COMPANY CONDOS NEXT TO THE PARK?

GOOD THING YOU DIDN'T BREAK A LEG. THERE'S NO NEED FOR STITCHES.

COME IN FOR A MINUTE. I'LL CLEAN UP YOUR WOUNDS.

HELLO.

OH...

23

HERE, YOU KEEP CLEANING IT.

AH...WHAT IS IT NOW?

AH HUH... NO.

I'M WITH A GIRL THAT YOU KNOW. AND IT'S ALL YOUR FAULT.

HAHA! WHAT ARE YOU TALKING ABOUT? I'M NOT FOOLING AROUND.

MMM-HMM.

I BETTER PUT THIS ON IN A HURRY AND LEAVE.

HONEST. YOU WANNA TALK TO HER?

......

HERE. IT'S YOUR FRIEND.

HELLO?

WHO IS THIS? SEY?! OH! YOU'RE WITH SIHO?!

WHY ISN'T YOUR CELL PHONE ON?

AH... UM... REA...WHAT HAPPENED, SEE, WAS...

Why am I stuttering? She'll think I'm trying to hide something!

AUTHOR'S NOTE: TELL ME YOUR OPINION OR COMPLAINTS ABOUT I.N.V.U. AT THE FOLLOWING WEBSITE: HTTP://MYHOME.NETSGO.COM/PHANTASMA. IT'S MY HOME PAGE.

Why am I suddenly feeling guilty towards Rea?

HE WAS TEACHING ME HOW TO SKATE...BUT...I GOT HURT...SO, I'M JUST NURSING MY WOUNDS.

OH, NO! SO YOU'RE AT SIHO'S PLACE? REALLY? THAT WAS QUICK. ARE YOU HURT BADLY?

SIHO IS A WIZ ON ROLLERBLADES.

GET THIS, I STILL DON'T KNOW HOW TO ROLLERBLADE. AND I'VE GOT THAT PART-TIME JOB, AND...

BY THE WAY... SIHO HAS A ROAMING HAND, IF YOU CATCH MY DRIFT. SO BE CAREFUL.

HOHOHO!

WHAT'S GOING ON?!

THAT JERK, HE BETTER NOT BE TWO-TIMING ME!

BUT...REA, ISN'T TWO-TIMING GUYS *YOUR* M.O?

WHY DID HE TAKE SEY TO HIS PLACE?

SHUT UP!

WAIT! NOW... IS THAT TWO-TIMING...OR QUADRUPLE-TIMING...?

Reality Check!

Introduction:

On the Virtual Internet System, no one knows you're a cat—even if you (sort of) look like one! When mild-mannered Collin Meeks' cat, Catreece, develops a taste for surfing the fully interactive VIS, Collin has his buffer full trying to keep her out of trouble! It's Super Information Hijinks as Collin and his paranoid friend Erk, along with Super Netgirl Maiko, meet up with playful Internet ghouls, super-encrypted virtual superheroes, and the ravenous Puffy Cat computer virus! It's a World Wide Web of goofy adventure in the not-so-distant future!

Created by:
Rikki Simons
and Tavisha
Wolfgarth-Simons

Release Date:
Vol. 01   Available Now
Vol. 02   05/13/03

Y
YOUTH
AGE 7+

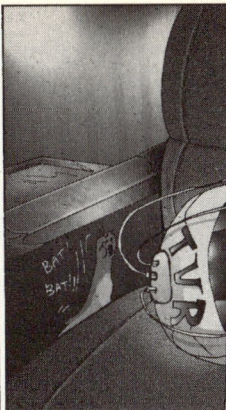

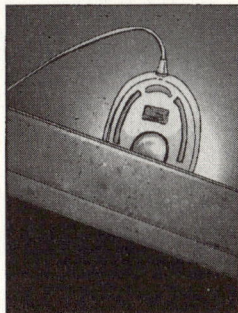

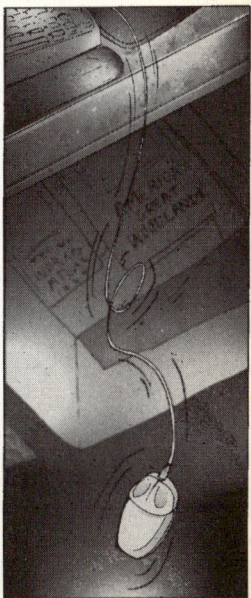

CONFIDENTIAL

TOKYOPOP **2003**
SNEAK PEEK SAMPLER

TOKYOPOP

LOS ANGELES · TOKYO · LONDON

TOKYOPOP 2003 SNEAK PEEK SAMPLER

<<< Right to Left

Table of Contents

Introduction

Congratulations on getting your hands on the ultra-exclusive TOKYOPOP 2003 Manga Sampler! As a sophisticated reader, you might notice there's something different about this book. It's manga done the authentic way.

Fans and creators have been demanding more authentic manga for years, and TOKYOPOP has been proud to answer that call with our 100% Authentic Manga. What does 100% Authentic Manga mean? Well, for fans, it means you get to see the artwork the way the author intended and not a mirror image. You see, most manga printed in America has been digitally flipped to make it read like American comics. This is all well and good until you realize that right-handed characters become left handed, cars drive on the wrong side of the road and all the words on signs, t-shirts and backgrounds are completely re-lettered. For creators, 100% Authentic Manga means their artwork is no longer covered up with awkward English sound effects and their carefully-planned layouts are no longer annoyingly reversed. Everyone wins! This sampler showcases ten TOKYOPOP manga series that read right-to-left.

For more information, visit us online at
www.TOKYOPOP.com

SHAOLIN 鈴 SISTERS

Created By:
Narumi Kakinouchi
Toshiki Hirano

Release Date:

Y
YOUTH
AGE 7+

Introduction:

Julin Kenga always thought that she was an only child and the sole heiress to the Fighting Fang martial arts clan. But after an unwarranted attack on her home destroys everything she holds dear, it comes as quite a surprise when her dying kung fu master gives her a magical bell and tells her to search for two older sisters she never knew existed!

Now she races to find them as the evil White Queen, Bai Wang, schemes to capture the three bells that the Kenga sisters hold. Nothing will stand in her way to unleash the true potential of the bells' power—nothing but the *Shaolin Sisters*, that is.

Shaolin Sisters was illustrated by one of Japan's most revered artists, Narumi Kakinouchi of *Vampire Princess Miyu* fame.

4

THE SHAOLIN STONE FIST...

WHY CAN'T I DO IT?

NOT EVEN NOW...

...WHEN I NEED IT MOST!

JULIN!

AH...

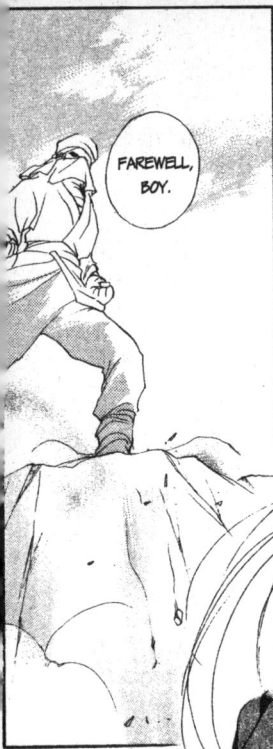

FAREWELL, BOY.

KIO!

AH...

KIO!

YOU'RE NEXT, LITTLE LADY.

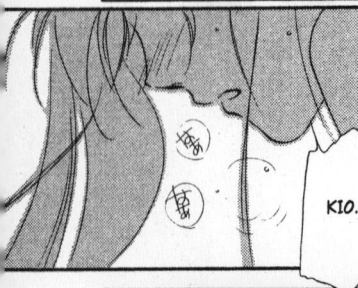

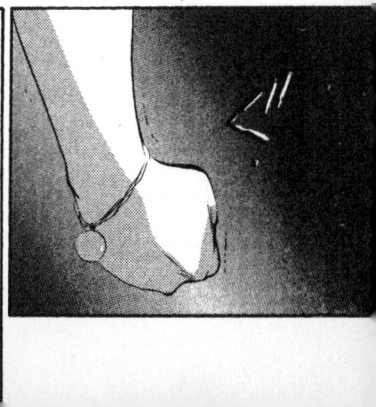

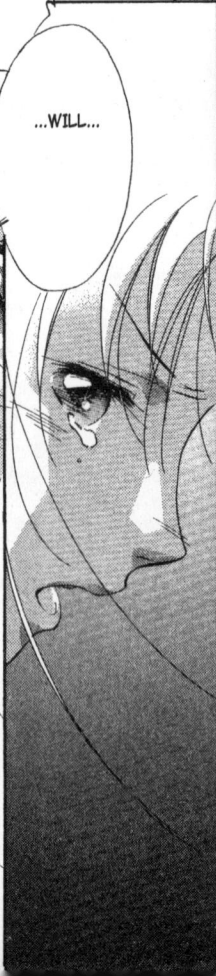

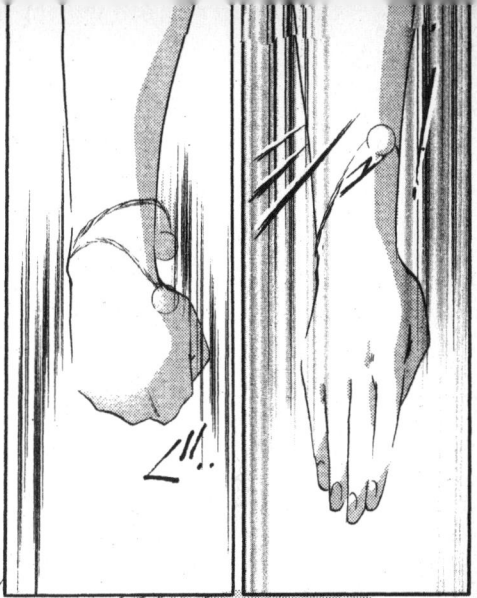

武硬拳
（ぶ）（こう）（けん）

...THE
SHAOLIN
STONE
FIST!

20 MENSO NI ONEGAI!

MAN OF MANY FACES

Created by:
CLAMP

Release Date:
Vol. 01   05/06/03
Vol. 02   07/15/03

Y
YOUTH
AGE 7+

Introduction:

Akira Ijyuin lives a double life. By day, he's a top student at the elite CLAMP School, but by night he's the infamous man with 20 faces. A master of disguise and stealth, this masked thief steals unusual objects at the whim of two devious crime lords—his two mothers! One starlit, night his routine is changed forever when he meets the lovely young Utako while hiding from the police. This time the tables are turned and Akira has something stolen from him—his heart.

Man of Many Faces is a coming-of-age romance that spans several years as a childhood crush turns into true love. It's filled with the comedy and cuteness that have made CLAMP one of the most popular manga creation teams in the world. With featured cameos from other CLAMP School characters, *Man of Many Faces* is a series no CLAMP fan will want to be without.

BRRRING

THERE HE IS!!

In our modern world, full of electronic surveillance and high-tech protection, a gentleman thief is a sensational creature.

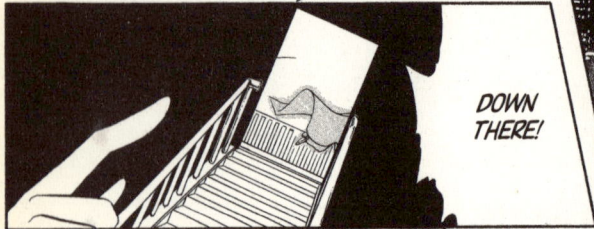

DOWN THERE!

HUH?!

This one's...

...the Mysterious Man with Twenty Faces.

EVENT

1

FIRST ENTRY
初登場

IT'S KIND OF MY UNOFFICIAL ALIAS.

AKIRA-SAAAAAAN!

AKIRA-SAN, IS BREAKFAST READY?

JUST A FEW MORE MINUTES!

I GO TO CLAMP SCHOOL. I'M IN THIRD GRADE.

MY NAME IS AKIRA IJYUIN.

IS THAT OKAY, OKA-SAN?

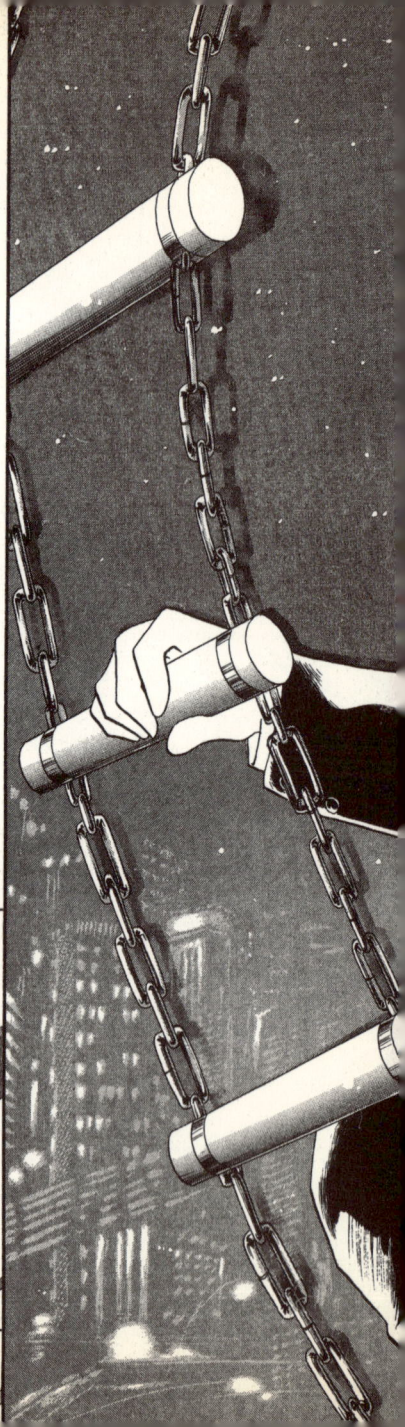

HE WAS THE ORIGINAL MAN OF MANY FACES.

I HAVE A FAVOR TO ASK, AKIRA-SAN.

THANK YOU!

I'VE NEVER MET MY OTOSAN.

I HAVE TWO OKASAN.

AKIRA-SAN, YOU ARE SUCH A CHEF!

DON'T BE SHY. DIG IN!

I HOPE IT WAS WORTH THE WAIT.

THE STAGE CURTAIN?

YES!

YOU KNOW THAT HUGE STAGE CURTAIN IN YOUR SCHOOL'S AUDITORIUM? THE REAL PRETTY ONE?

COULD YOU GET THAT FOR US?

THE PRINCIPAL IS REALLY PROUD OF ITS FINE QUALITY--

BUT THAT BELONGS TO THE SCHOOL.

HE'S OBSESSED WITH OUR LOCAL THIEF.

...AND HE'S GOT A PASSION FOR MYSTERIES.

OH, YEAH.

DID YOU HEAR? HE'S DONE IT AGAIN!

20 FACES ...?

HE'S A NICE GUY...

LET ME KNOW IF YOU NEED ANYTHING. YOU KNOW I'LL ALWAYS HELP.

YOU BET!!

OH.

HE WOULD BE SO SHOCKED TO KNOW I AM 20 FACES.

GOOD...

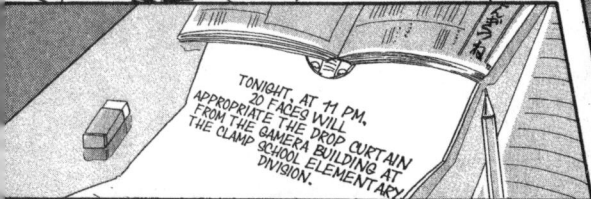

TONIGHT, AT 11 P.M., 20 FACES WILL APPROPRIATE THE DROP CURTAIN FROM THE GAMERA BUILDING AT THE CLAMP SCHOOL ELEMENTARY DIVISION.

WHAT A WEIRDO.

HIS NEXT TARGET IS THE CURTAIN FROM THE STAGE IN THE GAMERA BUILDING?

SO!!

THIS IS MY CHANCE TO CATCH HIM!

HEY, DUDE!

WAZZUP!

DID YOU HEAR THAT OL' 20 FACES HAS ANNOUNCED ANOTHER ONE?

IT'S GOING TO BE AT OUR SCHOOL!

tug tug

DO YOU HAVE A HANDKER-CHIEF?

THE BANANA WILL GIVE YOU POTASSIUM. (YES, I'M A FOOD NERD.)

HERE'S YOUR DINNER AND DESSERT!

23

THERE HE IS!

IT'S HEAVY!

UGH-ARGH.

UH-OH!

I KNEW STAKING THIS PLACE OUT WOULD WORK!

HE TOOK THE CURTAIN... JUST LIKE HE SAID!

HE'S HEADING TOWARD THE ROOF.

YOU SAW HIM? WHERE IS HE? WHERE?!

IT'S LATE. I'M SORRY TO HAVE KEPT YOU WAITING.

OH, THAT'S ALL RIGHT.

HMM...

THERE'S NO ESCAPE, 20 FACES!

I'D LOVE TO STAY AND CHAT, BUT IT'S PAST MY CURFEW.

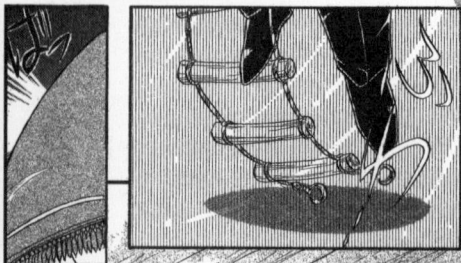

PARDON MY RUDENESS.

DON'T LET HIM GET AWAY! STOP HIM!!

IT'S NOT FAIR!

G' MORN-IN'!

HI, RYUSUKE-SAN!

SEE YOU TONIGHT!

WE HAD 20 FACES TRAPPED, AND HE GOT AWAY!

LAST NIGHT WAS A *DISASTER!*

I'M SORRY.

...AS A CARPET.

END

THE CURTAIN IS GOR-GEOUS...

WE MAY HAVE HAD TO BEG, BUT IT'S WORTH IT.

Tokyo MEW MEW

Created by:

Mia Ikumi

Reiko Yoshida

Release Date:

Vol. 01   Available Now

Vol. 02   06/17/03

Vol. 03   08/12/03

Vol. 04   10/14/03

Y

YOUTH
AGE 7+

Introduction:

Ichigo is out on a hot date with her crush when suddenly she's involved in an odd incident in which her DNA is merged with the DNA of an almost-extinct wildcat. When the DNA of four other girls is also merged with the DNA of four other nearly-extinct animals, it's apparent that they're part of a much bigger plan. Ichigo and her friends have been chosen to become a part of a secret initiative called the "Mew Project." Their mission: To protect the planet from aliens who are using the world's animals to attack humans. Only time will tell if these supernatural superheroes will be up to the challenge.

IT'S SO NICE OUTSIDE TODAY...

Endangered Species Exhibition

Earth-
A beautiful blue
filled with mil
of life form
-Earth

SIGH!

HUH? OH, SURE!

HEY, ICHIGO, TAKE A LOOK!

SO WHY AM I STUCK IN AN ENDANGERED SPECIES EXHIBIT?!

He's flashing such a cute smile at that display...

WE HAVE SO MANY ENDANGERED SPECIES ON OUR PLANET.

I wish he'd flash that smile at me.

SOB!

I DIDN'T EXPECT YOU TO...

OH, UM, I THINK IT'S SO IMPORTANT TO SAVE THE PLANET!

HUH?

I WANTED TO KNOW MORE ABOUT YOU...

...INVITE ME TO THE ENDANGERED SPECIES EXHIBIT.

I AGREE.

Yes!

He's so cute!

HE'S SMART, HE'S CUTE...

HE'S VERY ATHLETIC.

AND POPULAR AT SCHOOL BUT...

basketball player

WHAT I LIKE BEST IS HIS SMILE!!

Twinkle, Twinkle

Even if this is just a boring exhibit in a gloomy museum...

I don't care where I am... as long as we're together.

LET'S GO CHECK OUT THE WOLVES.

SURE!

31

HUH? WAIT A SEC, ICHIGO.

OKAY.

LET'S GO SEE WHAT'S NEXT!

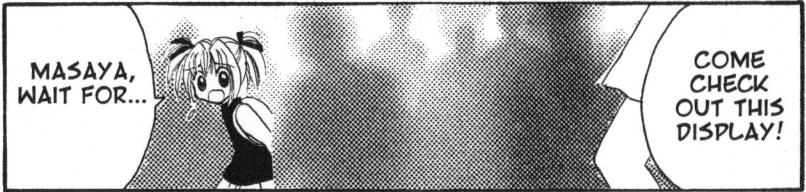

MASAYA, WAIT FOR...

COME CHECK OUT THIS DISPLAY!

...ME.

NOOO!

WHOA!

UH-OH.

ICHIGO?!

WHAT?

32

I WASN'T EXPECTING TO KISS HIM...

I ALWAYS WANTED TO HOLD HANDS WITH HIM, BUT...

I'M SO SORRY... DO YOU HAVE SOME TISSUES?

ICHIGO!

Maybe he likes me!

What is it?

MASAYA...

I JUST THOUGHT...

GIGGLE

WASTING TISSUE PAPER LEADS TO DEFORESTATION.

YES?

PLEASE, USE THIS.

THANK YOU...

WE'RE OKAY.

OH, NO!

THIS HANKIE IS MADE FROM RECYCLED FIBERS!

WHAT NOW?!?

MASAYA,

SEE THIS?

What was her sneer about?

BEAUTIFUL!

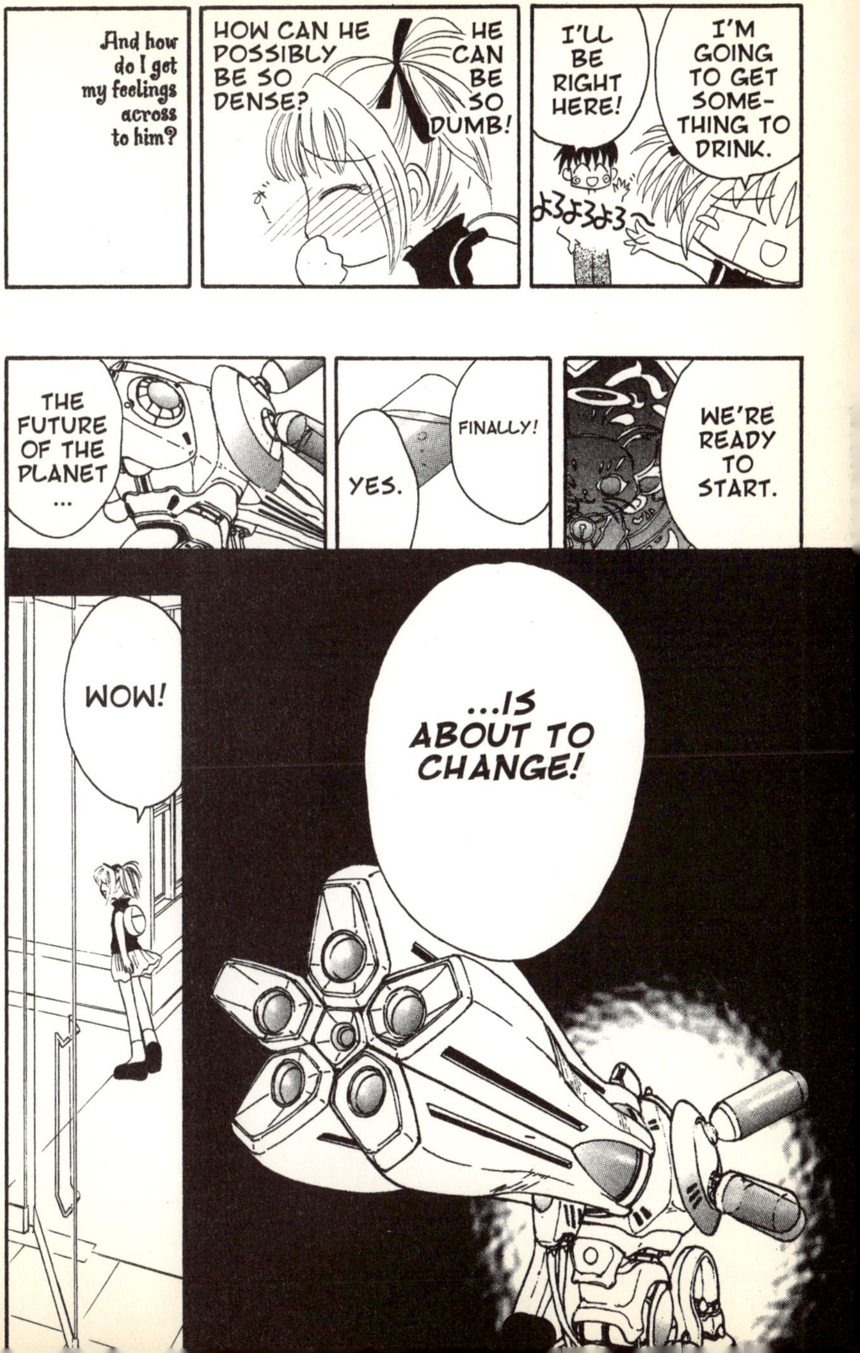
I'M GOING TO GET SOME-THING TO DRINK.
I'LL BE RIGHT HERE!
よろよろよろ〜
HE CAN BE SO DUMB!
HOW CAN HE POSSIBLY BE SO DENSE?
And how do I get my feelings across to him?
WE'RE READY TO START.
FINALLY!
YES.
THE FUTURE OF THE PLANET ...
...IS ABOUT TO CHANGE!
WOW!

Project Meeting 1

CAN YOU TAKE A LOOK AT THIS PLAN?

OH, SURE ...

Bio-engineered
Warriors of Justice

Bio-engineered
Warriors of Justice

THIS TITLE MUST BE A JOKE, RIGHT?

NO, WE SPENT HOURS ON THAT TITLE!!

WHAT A CUTE CAFE!

COOL. I NEVER KNEW THAT WAS HERE.

MAYBE I'LL ASK MASAYA TO TAKE ME THERE AFTER THIS.

And maybe things could get romantic!

WHAT?

OH...

TRUE LOVE CAN BE SO DIFFI-CULT!

IT'S ...

IT'S SARCASM GIRL!! SHE'S BACK!

HAVE YOU BEEN SPYING ON US OR SOMETHING?

WELL...

HE MUST BE SO DENSE!

IT'S SO OBVIOUS THAT YOU HAVE A CRUSH ON HIM.

THIS IS NONE OF YOUR BUSINESS.

How lame!

WHAT!?

YOU TWO ARE A BIT MORE INTERESTING THAN THESE DISPLAYS.

YOU'RE SO STUPID!

WHAT'S GOING ON?

YOU'RE STARTING TO TICK ME OFF!

YOU'VE BEEN NOTHING BUT SARCASTIC AND RUDE.

YEAH... YOU'RE TICK-ING...

REBOUND

Created by:

Yuriko Nishiyama

Release Date:

Vol. 01	Available Now
Vol. 02	06/17/03
Vol. 03	08/05/03
Vol. 04	10/07/03
Vol. 05	12/09/03

Introduction:

The Johnan High School basketball team has worked hard all year and has finally found themselves contenders at the National Interhigh Basketball Championships in Sapporo. But their success at clobbering teams in their small pond back home did not prepare them to face the top-notch talent of the Championships. It's going to take a lot of teamwork—and a lot of faith in themselves—to emerge victorious. *Rebound*—the sequel to TOKYOPOP's *Harlem Beat*—reunites the old Scratch and Johnan teams and takes them to new heights.

THE ONLY GUYS PLAYING WORTH A LICK...

...ARE SHURMAN AND KOBAYASHI.

WHAT'S HAPPENED TO THEIR COOL DEMEANOR?

THEY CAN'T CONCENTRATE.

THE MORE THEY SWEAT, THE CRAZIER THEY GET.

UNG

OH!

UMMPFF

HE'S AUTOMATIC.

JOHNAN AT THE FREE-THROW LINE AGAIN!

FOCUS, KOBAYASHI.

THAT REF'S TOUGH... THAT COULD HAVE GONE EITHER WAY.

OKINAWA'S NOT GETTING ANY BREAKS.

BLOCKING, NUMBER 8, OKINAWA.

JUST RAISE YOUR HAND!

WHAT ARE YOU, BLIND?

41

THEY SINK THE THREE!
KYAN FAKES THE DRIVE AND DISHES OUTSIDE FOR THE THREE!
TIME-OUT JOHNAN
GET THE TOWELS.
OKAY.
ALL DUNKS AND HARD FOULS. THESE GUYS ARE TOUGH!
YEAH.
THIS IS DEFINITELY THEIR PACE.
TCH
I CAN'T KEEP UP LIKE THIS.
WELL, COMPLAINING WON'T SLOW THEM DOWN.
THEY'VE GOT US ON THE RUN.
WE NEED TO ADMIT TO OURSELVES THAT WE JUST CAN'T KEEP UP.

ONE VAMPIRE'S SEARCH FOR
Revenge and Redemption...

REBIRTH

By: Kang-Woo Lee

Joined by
an excommunicated
exorcist and a
spiritual investigator,
Deshwitat begins
his bloodquest.
The hunted is
now the hunter.

TOKYOPOP

GET REBIRTH VOL. 1
IN YOUR FAVORITE BOOK & COMIC STORES NOW!

VOL. 2 AVAILABLE MAY 2003

T TEEN AGE 13+

www.TOKYOPOP.com

happy mania

Created by:

Moyoco Anno

Release Date:

M MATURE AGES 18+

Introduction:

The misadventures of one young woman in search of love and a relationship take center stage in *Happy Mania*, a revolutionary new shojo manga series. The 24-year-old Shigeta spends her days working at Tanaka Books and fretting over her love life or—more accurately—her lack thereof. The biggest obstacle to finding a satisfying relationship seems to be Shigeta herself. When it comes to men, this poor girl has exceedingly poor judgment, exacerbated by her even poorer self-esteem. It's hard to imagine she could respect anyone who actually finds her attractive. They say love happens when you least expect it—but if you're obsessed with it 24/7, then what? Join Shigeta and her gal pals in their hilarious hunt for love, romance, and together-forever commitment.

MY MOTHER AND MY ROOMMATE CAME TO PICK ME
UP WHEN I GOT OUT OF THE HOSPITAL.

THANK YOU
SO MUCH
FOR EVERY-
THING!

I STILL DON'T
HAVE A
BOYFRIEND!

....

I FORGOT THAT I CAN'T DEAL WITH THE TYPE OF CHEESEBALL GUYS THAT COME TO THESE PLACES.

I CAN'T... I CAN'T DO THIS...

HEY, FUKU, IT'S BEEN A WHILE.

HEY, HOW ARE YOU?

WHAT? I CAN'T HEAR YOU.

THERE ARE A LOT OF YOUNG PEOPLE HERE, BUT NOT MANY GUYS.

I'M GOING HOME TO SLEEP!

AND I'M WEARING A "GUARANTEED GUY-FRIENDLY" SEE-THROUGH SHIRT, ACCORDING TO COSMO MAGAZINE...

WHAT!? I CAN'T HEAR YOU.

FUKU, I'M GOING HOME.

YOU'RE GOING HOME?

I'M NOT GOING TO MEET SOMEONE IN THIS PLACE... IT'S NOT THAT EASY.

AND AGAIN, AND AGAIN...

BESIDES, I'LL JUST WAKE UP ALONE AGAIN.

SEE YA.

GOOD NIGHT.

I HEARD ABOUT THAT, TOO.

I COULDN'T GO UP TO HIM IN THE CLUB...

...SO NOW I'M HERE. AM I A STALKER?

JAPANESE STYLE COMPANY

LIGHT

TAXI

-FAKE-

Created by:

Sanami Matoh

Release Date:

Vol. 01   05/06/03
Vol. 02   07/08/03
Vol. 03   09/09/03
Vol. 04   11/04/03

OT
OLDER TEEN
AGE 16+

Fake

Introduction:

Sanami Matoh's *FAKE*—a shonen-ai favorite—is an unlikely love story between two NYC cops who both happen to be guys. Meet Ryo and Dee, two New York City cops with an attraction for action—and each other! When Ryo, a soft spoken officer, joins the NYPD's 27th precinct, he's soon partnered up with Dee—a cocky, confident cop with attitude to spare. Soon, Dee reveals his feelings for Ryo run much deeper than friendship, but, at first, Ryo isn't exactly receptive to his overtures. In fact, he's not sure what to think or where to turn! Before long, their attention is diverted by a myriad of crimes to solve and criminals to catch. As the authoritative officers obliterate crime in the streets of the gritty city, their bond grows stronger and stronger. Soon, it's impossible to ignore the electrified emotions that are brewing between them. Could this be love?!

HIS OFFICE IS THE ONE RIGHT AT THE END OF THAT HALL OVER THERE.

NOW YOU JUST NEED TO CHECK IN WITH THE INVESTIGATION CHIEF.

OKAY, YOU'RE ALL SET HERE.

UMMM, YEAH. I'LL BE SURE TO DO THAT, JANET.

THANKS.

YOU'RE VERY WELCOME.

OH, AND, UH, BY THE WAY, RANDY— JUST DON'T FORGET TO ASK ME OUT SOME TIME WHEN YOU'RE FREE, OKAY?

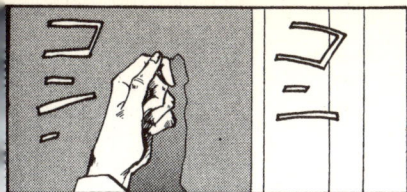

HOPE THIS IS IT.

AND HERE WE ARE... RIGHT AT THE END OF THE HALL.

!?

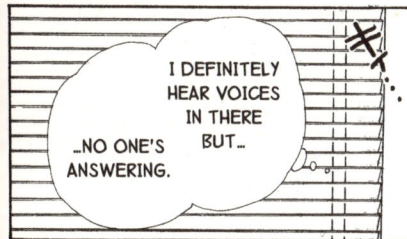

I DEFINITELY HEAR VOICES IN THERE BUT...

...NO ONE'S ANSWERING.

TOO WEIRD.

YOU IDIOT!

ACK!

HEY,
ROOKIE.

IT'S
RANDY,
SIR.

3"

YOU'RE
NOT GOING
ANYWHERE!

WELL, YOU'RE
OBVIOUSLY A BIT BUSY,
SO I THOUGHT IT
WOULD BE IN YOUR
BEST INTEREST IF I
RETURNED TO MY
INVESTIGATORY
DUTIES, SIR,
AND...

ALL RIGHT,
RANDY...

Give
it up.

!!

ASK HIM
TO SHOW
YOU THE
ROPES.

MEET
YOUR NEW
PARTNER.

Just don't
do anything
stupid like
following
his example.

...MISTER
LAYTNER.

Y'KNOW, I'D
APPRECIATE IF
YOU'D RETRACT
THAT 'CHILD'
COMMENT...

Child!?

WWHAAA~!?

W-WHY THE
HECK DO I
GET STUCK
TAKING CARE
OF THE NEW
CHILD, HUH?!

HAVE FUN,
KID.
REMEMBER
TO TAKE
GOOD CARE
OF HIM.

68

So you wanna be
a Rock 'n' Roll star...

Gravitation

by Maki Murakami

100% AUTHENTIC MANGA

Rock 'n' Roll & manga collide with superstar
dreams in this hit property from Japan!

VOL. 1 IN YOUR FAVORITE
BOOK & COMIC STORES NOW!

T TEEN AGE 13+

www.TOKYOPOP.com

BATTLE ROYALE

KOUSHUN TAKAMI & MASAYUKI TAGUCHI

Created by:
Koushun Takami
Masayuki Taguchi

English Adaptation:
Keith Giffen

Release Date:
Vol. 01   05/13/03
Vol. 02   07/15/03
Vol. 03   09/16/03
Vol. 04   11/11/03

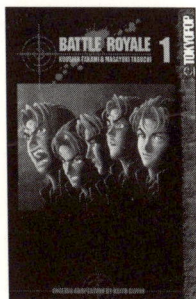

M
MATURE
AGES 18+

Introduction:

In the dark, morally-bankrupt future society dreamed up by Takami and Taguchi, there's a national lottery. But in this lottery, there's no multimillion-dollar check to turn your life around. "Winners" of the lottery compete in "The Program"—a game show that picks a random ninth-grade class and puts the students on an abandoned island for a televised fight to the death. Only one can be left alive. *Battle Royale* has attracted an incredible cult following in Japan. Is America ready for it? Are you ready for it? TOKYOPOP brings you this groundbreaking series featuring an English adaptation by renowned writer Keith Giffen. Put aside your morals, hold onto your seats and prepare yourself for an unforgettable manga experience. Prepare yourself for *BATTLE ROYALE!*

Based on Koushun Takami's best-selling book and movie of the same name.

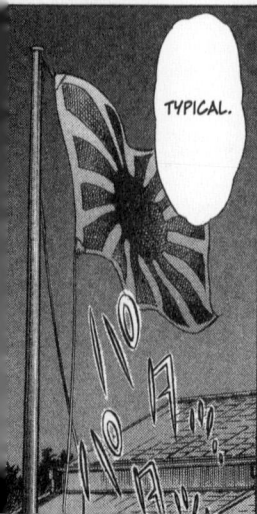

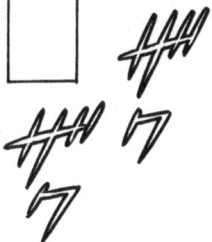

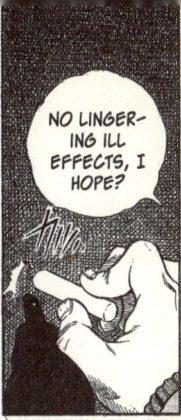

?
IS THIS GUY SERIOUS?
COMPETITION? LIKE A GAME?
GET REAL!
SO ...
I THINK YOU'LL FIND THE NEXT FEW DAYS... INTERESTING, TO SAY THE LEAST.
SOME AMONG YOU MIGHT EVEN "GET OFF ON IT," TO USE THE VERNACULAR.
IT'S ALL A MATTER OF PERSONAL PREFERENCE.
stomp
SOME OPT FOR FOOLHARDY COURAGE, OTHERS, DELIBERATE CAUTION.
STILL OTHERS, CRAVEN COWARDICE.
THERE ARE STOIC LONERS AND THOSE WHO FIND STRENGTH IN NUMBERS.
skritch
I WOULD ADVISE AGAINST THAT EXCEPT AS A TEMPORARY NECESSITY.
?
YES...
FRIENDS, I'M SORRY TO SAY, ALL TOO SOON BECOME LIABILITIES. TRUST, FRAGILE.
THIS... IT CAN'T BE...
SANITY, EVEN MORE FRAGILE.
AH, AH... I NEVER SAID IT WOULD BE EASY.

FORTY-TWO
COMPETE UNTIL
A WINNER IS
DETERMINED.

SURVIVAL
OF THE FITTEST...
OR SO WE LIKE
TO BELIEVE.

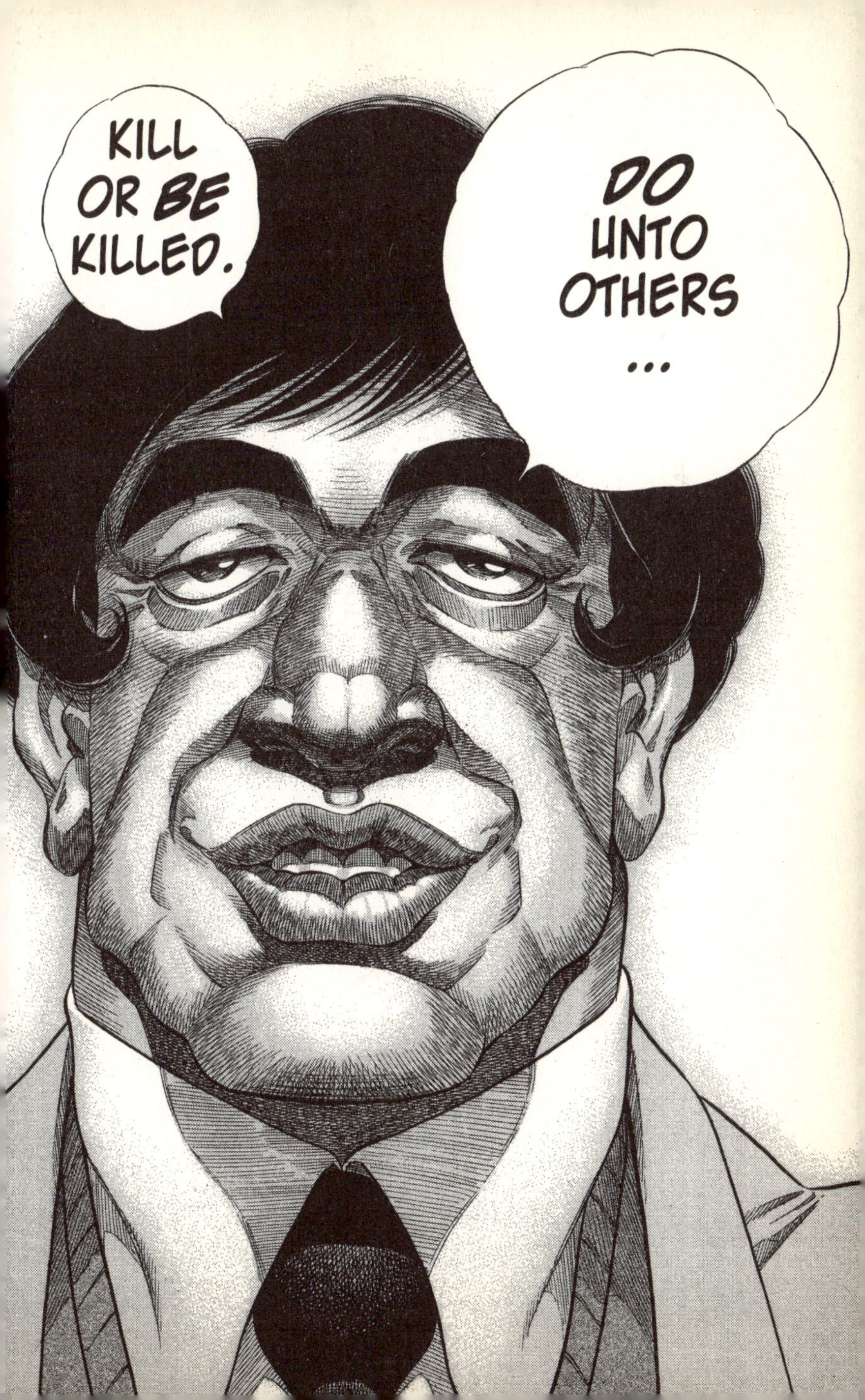
DO UNTO OTHERS ...
KILL OR BE KILLED.

SAMURAI DEEPER KYO

100% AUTHENTIC MANGA

BY: AKIMINE KAMIJYO

The Action-Packed Samurai Drama that Spawned the Hit Anime!

Slice the surface
to find the assassin within...

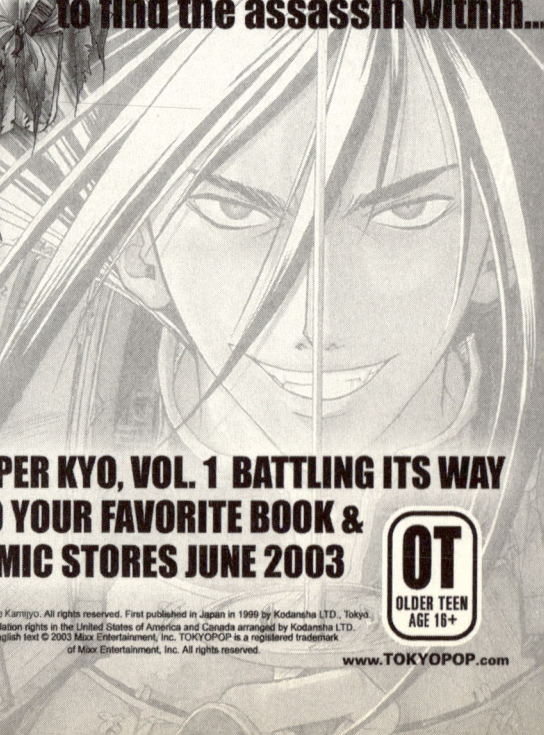

SAMURAI DEEPER KYO, VOL. 1 BATTLING ITS WAY
INTO YOUR FAVORITE BOOK &
COMIC STORES JUNE 2003

OT
OLDER TEEN
AGE 16+

www.TOKYOPOP.com

erica
SAKURAZAWA

between the sheets

Created by:
Erica Sakurazawa

Release Dates:
Between The Sheets
05/06/03

Angel:
07/08/2003

Angel Nest:
09/09/2003

Nothing But
Loving You:
11/04/2003

Rules of Love:
01/13/2004

Aromatic Bitters:
03/04/2004

Introduction:

Welcome to Sex and the City, manga-style, in this sophisticated chick-lit series from acclaimed manga-ka Erica Sakurazawa. In Between the Sheets, Sakurazawa delves into the best friendship of Minako and Saki. Minako likes her best friend Saki because she is free, wild and uninhibited. Over time, her feelings for Saki slowly evolve way beyond friendship. Between the Sheets depicts Minako's bittersweet experiences as she falls deeper and deeper in love with her best friend, Saki. TOKYOPOP is proud to publish, for the first time in English, six of Sakurazawa's most compelling and provocative works, each of which explore a different topic and can stand alone. These fairy tales for adults are lovingly drawn and feature elements of magic and mystery, as well as some gritty realism drawn from daily metropolitan life in our times.

LET'S GO TO CLUB YELLOW NEXT SATURDAY.

I'VE HEARD THEY HAVE AN AWESOME DJ.

OH, DON'T WORRY ABOUT HIM. HE'LL SURVIVE A NIGHT WITHOUT ME.

BUT I THOUGHT SATURDAY WAS THE ONLY NIGHT YOU COULD SPEND WITH KEN.

all ¥1000

ABSOLUTELY, NO PROBLEM.

DAMN, YOU'RE SO CONFIDENT! ARE YOU SURE IT'S OKAY?

THE MOST CRUCIAL THING IN A RELATIONSHIP IS HAVING CONTROL OVER YOUR BOYFRIEND.
AH, I GET IT.
BUT I CAN NEVER BE AS COOL AS YOU ARE, SAKI.
I'M ALWAYS SO WORRIED ABOUT WHETHER THE GUY STILL LIKES ME OR NOT.
I OBSESS OVER HIS FEELINGS 24/7...
...AND I END UP BEING ONE OF THOSE PATHETIC, WHIPPED "WOMEN WHO LOVE TOO MUCH."

LET'S COOK IT TOGETHER. I'LL HELP.

THAT'S SO LAME! WE HAD PLANS TO COOK DINNER TOGETHER TONIGHT.

OKAY.

WHAT AM I SUPPOSED TO DO WITH ALL THIS FOOD?

DAMN, SAKI BLEW ME OFF!

HEY, DO YOU REALIZE...

KARE KANO, VOL. 5
LIZZIE MCGUIRE CINE-MANGA RUMORS AND
  JACK OF ALL TRADES, VOL.2
LUPIN III, VOL. 7
PRIEST, VOL. 8
SABER MARIONETTE J, VOL. 2
STRAY SHEEP FIND A SHAPE, VOL. 7
STRAY SHEEP MERRY ON THE MOVE, VOL. 3
STRAY SHEEP HIDE AND SEEK, VOL. 4
STRAY SHEEP COUNT TO SLEEP, VOL. 5
STRAY SHEEP POE AT PLAY, VOL. 2
STRAY SHEEP PICK A SHADE, VOL. 6
STRAY SHEEP PICTURE BOOK, VOL. 1
WILD ACT, VOL. 2
ZODIAC P.I., VOL. 2
BABY BIRTH, VOL. 1
BATTLE ROYALE, VOL. 3
DUKLYON: CLAMP SCHOOL DEFENDERS, VOL. 1
FLCL, VOL. 1
GTO, VOL. 14
JACKIE CHAN ADVENTURES, VOL. 1
JIMMY NEUTRON, VOL. 1
KIM POSSIBLE CINE-MANGA, VOL. 3
KODOCHA: SANA'S STAGE, VOL. 9
LIZZIE MCGUIRE CINE-MANGA, VOL. 3
LOVE HINA, VOL. 14
MARS, VOL. 14
PEACH GIRL: CHANGE OF HEART, VOL. 4
REBIRTH, VOL. 4
SCRYED, VOL. 4
SPONGEBOB SQUAREPANTS, VOL. 1
UNDER THE GLASS MOON, VOL. 2

OCTOBER RELEASES
CHOBITS, VOL. 8
DRAGON HUNTER, VOL. 3
DRAGON KNIGHTS, VOL. 10
FORBIDDEN DANCE, VOL. 2
G GUNDAM, VOL. 3
GRAVITATION, VOL. 3
INITIAL D, VOL. 8
KING OF HELL, VOL.3
LUPIN III, VOL. 8
MIYUKI-CHAN IN WONDERLAND, VOL. 1
PLANETES, VOL. 1
RAGNAROK, VOL. 8
REBOUND, VOL. 4
THE KINDAICHI CASE FILES DEATH TV, VOL. 3
BRAIN POWERED, VOL. 3
BRIGADOON, VOL. 2
HAPPY MANIA, VOL. 4
JING: KING OF BANDITS, VOL. 3
KARMA CLUB, VOL. 2
MAGIC KNIGHT RAYEARTH , VOL. 2
NIEA_7, VOL. 2
PET SHOP OF HORRORS , VOL. 3
RAVE MASTER, VOL. 5
SAMURAI DEEPER KYO, VOL. 3
SHAOLIN SISTERS, VOL. 5
TOKYO MEW MEW, VOL. 4
VAMPIRE GAME, VOL. 3
X-DAY, VOL. 2

NOVEMBER RELEASES
BABY BIRTH, VOL. 2
CHRONICLES OF THE CURSED SWORD, VOL. 3
CONFIDENTIAL CONFESSIONS, VOL. 3
DEMON DIARY, VOL. 4
ERICA SAKURAZAWA: NOTHING BUT LOVING YOU, VOL. 1
ESCAFLOWNE, VOL. 3
FAKE, VOL. 4
FLCL, VOL. 2
JACKIE CHAN ADVENTURES, VOL. 2
LUPIN III, VOL. 9
POWER RANGERS 'NINJA STORM' CINE-MANGA, VOL.2
PRIEST, VOL. 9
REBIRTH, VOL. 5
SABER MARIONETTE J, VOL. 3
SCRYED, VOL. 5
WILD ACT, VOL. 3
ZODIAC P.I., VOL. 3
BATTLE ROYALE, VOL. 4
DUKLYON: CLAMP SCHOOL DEFENDERS, VOL. 2
GTO, VOL. 15
I.N.V.U., VOL. 4
KARE KANO, VOL. 6
KODOCHA: SANA'S STAGE, VOL. 10
MARS, VOL. 15
PARADISE KISS, VOL. 5
PEACH GIRL: CHANGE OF HEART, VOL. 5
SHUTTERBOX, VOL. 2
SPONGEBOB SQUAREPANTS, VOL. 2

DECEMBER RELEASES
DRAGON KNIGHTS, VOL. 11
GRAVITATION, VOL. 4
HAPPY MANIA, VOL. 5
INITIAL D, VOL. 9
JING: KING OF BANDITS, VOL. 4
KIM POSSIBLE CINE-MANGA, VOL. 4
LIZZIE MCGUIRE CINE-MANGA, VOL. 4
LUPIN III, VOL. 10
MAGIC KNIGHT RAYEARTH, VOL. 3
RAVE MASTER, VOL. 6
REBOUND, VOL. 5
SAMURAI DEEPER KYO, VOL. 4
SHIRAHIME-SYO: SNOW GODDESS TALES, VOL. 1
THE KINDAICHI CASE FILES SMOKE AND MIRRORS, VOL. 4
ZODIAC P.I., VOL. 4

2003 RELEASE SCHEDULE

MAY RELEASES
DEMON DIARY, VOL. 1
ERICA SAKURAZAWA: BETWEEN THE SHEETS, VOL. 1
FAKE, VOL. 1
GATE KEEPERS, VOL. 2
REBIRTH DISPLAY FOR MAY, 2003
KARE KANO, VOL. 3
KODOCHA: SANA'S STAGE, VOL. 7
LIZZIE MCGUIRE CINE-MANGA
  POOL PARTY AND PICTURE DAY, VOL. 1
LOVE HINA, VOL. 10
MAN OF MANY FACES, VOL. 1
PRIEST, VOL. 6
REBIRTH, VOL. 2
BATTLE ROYALE, VOL. 1
DIGIMON, VOL. 2
GTO, VOL. 11
I.N.V.U., VOL. 2
MARS, VOL. 10
MIRACLE GIRLS, VOL. 9
PEACH GIRL: CHANGE OF HEART, VOL. 2
REALITY CHECK, VOL. 2
RISING STARS OF MANGA, VOL. 1
SCRYED, VOL. 2
THE SKULL MAN, VOL. 6

JUNE RELEASES
CARDCAPTOR SAKURA - MASTER OF THE CLOW, VOL. 5
CHOBITS, VOL. 6
COWBOY BEBOP: SHOOTING STAR, VOL. 2
DIGIMON, VOL. 3
DRAGON HUNTER, VOL. 1
DRAGON KNIGHTS, VOL. 8
GRAVITATION, VOL. 1
HAPPY MANIA, VOL. 2
JING: KING OF BANDITS, VOL. 1
KIM POSSIBLE CINE-MANGA
  MONKEY FIST STRIKES AND ATTACK
  OF THE KILLER BEBES, VOL. 2
KING OF HELL, VOL. 1
LOVE HINA, VOL. 11
LUPIN III, VOL. 4
SAMURAI DEEPER KYO, VOL. 1
THE KINDAICHI CASE FILES
  THE OPERA HOUSE MURDERS, VOL. 1
UNDER THE GLASS MOON, VOL. 1
BRAIN POWERED, VOL. 1
CLAMP SCHOOL DETECTIVES, VOL. 2
G GUNDAM, VOL. 1
GTO, VOL. 12
INITIAL D, VOL. 6
MARMALADE BOY, VOL. 7
MARS, VOL. 11
PET SHOP OF HORRORS, VOL. 1
RAVE MASTER, VOL. 3
REBOUND, VOL. 2
SHAOLIN SISTERS, VOL. 3
TOKYO MEW MEW, VOL. 2
VAMPIRE GAME, VOL. 1

JULY RELEASES
CONFIDENTIAL CONFESSIONS, VOL. 1
DEMON DIARY, VOL. 2
ERICA SAKURAZAWA: ANGEL, VOL. 1
ESCAFLOWNE, VOL. 1
FAKE, VOL. 2

KARE KANO, VOL. 4
LOVE HINA, VOL. 12
LUPIN III, VOL. 5
PRIEST, VOL. 7
SABER MARIONETTE J, VOL. 1
WILD ACT, VOL. 1
ZODIAC P.I., VOL. 1
BATTLE ROYALE, VOL. 2
CHRONICLES OF THE CURSED SWORD, VOL. 1
DIGIMON, VOL. 4
KARMA CLUB: THE CASE OF THE GREEN GOO, VOL. 1
KODOCHA: SANA'S STAGE, VOL. 8
MAN OF MANY FACES, VOL. 2
MARS, VOL. 12
PEACH GIRL: CHANGE OF HEART, VOL. 3
RAGNAROK, VOL. 7
REBIRTH, VOL. 3
SCRYED, VOL.3

AUGUST RELEASES
@LARGE, VOL. 1
CARDCAPTOR SAKURA -
  MASTER OF THE CLOW, VOL. 6
CHOBITS, VOL. 7
DRAGON HUNTER, VOL. 2
DRAGON KNIGHTS, VOL. 9
FORBIDDEN DANCE, VOL. 1
G GUNDAM, VOL. 2
GRAVITATION, VOL. 2
INITIAL D, VOL. 7
JING: KING OF BANDITS, VOL. 2
KING OF HELL, VOL. 2
LUPIN III, VOL. 6
MAGIC KNIGHT RAYEARTH I, VOL. 1
MARMALADE BOY, VOL. 8
POWER RANGERS 'NINJA STORM'
  CINE-MANGA, VOL. 1
REBOUND, VOL. 3
SHUTTERBOX, VOL. 1
WORLD OF HARTZ, VOL. 1
BRAIN POWERED, VOL. 2
BRIGADOON, VOL. 1
CLAMP SCHOOL DETECTIVES, VOL 3
DIGIMON, VOL. 5
GTO, VOL. 13
HAPPY MANIA, VOL. 3
I.N.V.U., VOL. 3
LOVE HINA, VOL. 13
MARS, VOL. 13
NIEA_7, VOL. 1
PET SHOP OF HORRORS, VOL. 2
RAVE MASTER, VOL. 4
SAMURAI DEEPER KYO, VOL. 2
SHAOLIN SISTERS, VOL. 4
THE KINDAICHI CASE FILES THE MUMMY'S CURSE, VOL. 2
THE SKULL MAN, VOL. 7
TOKYO MEW MEW, VOL. 3
VAMPIRE GAME, VOL. 2
X-DAY, VOL. 1
SEPTEMBER RELEASES
CHRONICLES OF THE CURSED SWORD, VOL. 2
CONFIDENTIAL CONFESSIONS, VOL. 2
DEMON DIARY, VOL. 3
ERICA SAKURAZAWA: ANGEL NEST, VOL. 1
ESCAFLOWNE, VOL. 2
FAKE, VOL. 3

KWEEE!!

DR. RED-FIELD!!

IT'S TOO LATE FOR HIM!! I'VE GOT YOU COVERED, RUN!!

GAAH!!

UMPH!!

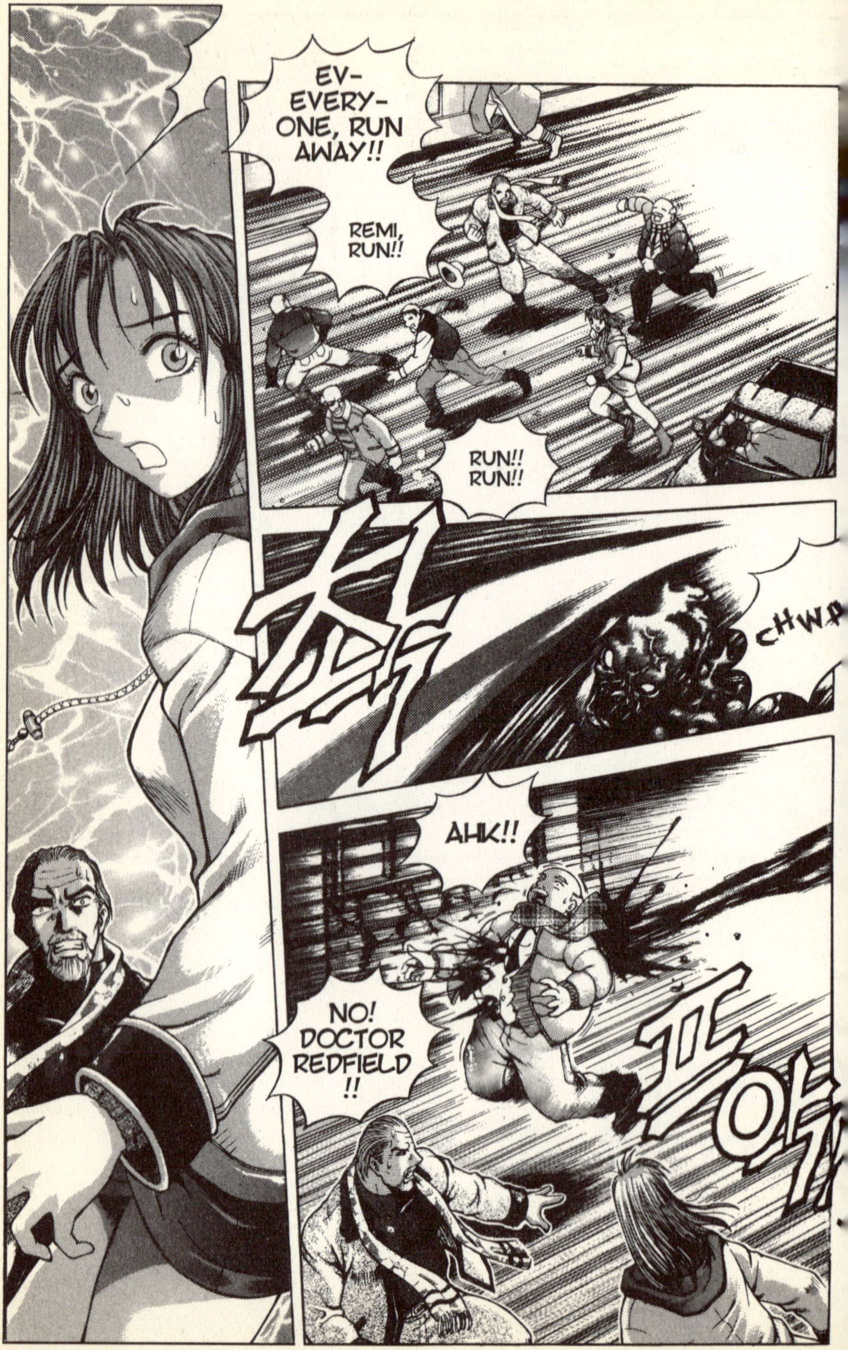
EV-
EVERY-
ONE, RUN
AWAY!!
REMI,
RUN!!
RUN!!
RUN!!
AHK!!
NO!
DOCTOR
REDFIELD
!!

MONSTER!!

THEY WERE RIGHT BELOW US!!

AUTHOR'S NOTE:
Laknes (level 4)

Underworld/undead/earth dweller

A traditional servant of zombies, they live buried underground. Their legs are badly atrophied, so they walk very slowly. To counter this, the Laknes can lengthen its arms at will. Fear of light usually confines them to appearing at night or on days of heavy overcast. Human flesh is their primary diet. Laknes are not very intelligent, but possess a powerful natural ferocity.

LOOK! I'M DETECTING A STEADY INCREASE IN ENER-GY!!

OHHH... AND IT'S NOT JUST ONE OR TWO SIG-NATURES... IT'S INCREDIBLE!

HMM... BUT THERE'S SOMETHING A LITTLE *STRANGE* ABOUT ALL THIS.

ASSUMING THAT YOUR DEVICE IS FUNCTIONING PROPERLY, IT'S DETECTING 5 OR 6 ENERGY SIGNATURES...

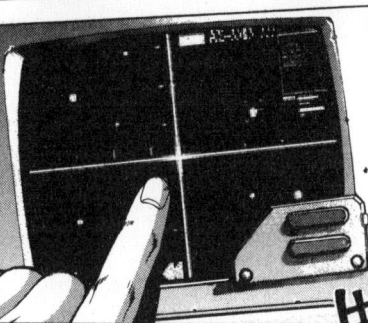

...AND OF THOSE, THIS ONE'S SIGNATURE IS UNUSUALLY STRONG.

FURTHER-MORE...

...IF THESE COORDI-NATES ARE CORRECT, THE ENERGY IS COMING FROM THE EXACT POINT WE'RE STANDING ON!

YOU HAVEN'T FIGURED IT OUT? THE EXPLA-NATION'S OBVI-OUS!

THE BRIGHT FLASHY LIGHT IS THE LEADER AND...

BUT THERE'S NOTHING HERE. DOESN'T THAT SEEM A LITTLE... ODD?

GRRR... WHO ASKED YOU!!

...WE CAN'T SEE THEM BECAUSE THEY'RE EITHER ABOVE US...

JEEZ... WHY IN THE WORLD DID I AGREE TO COME WITH YOU? I'M WASTING MY PRECIOUS WINTER VACATION!
I FEEL LIKE I'M TAKING A FIELD TRIP WITH A BUNCH OF KINDERGARTNERS...
...ANYWAYS...
THE ATMOSPHERE AROUND HERE SURE IS STRANGE...
...IT REALLY FEELS LIKE A VAMPIRE MIGHT BE LIVING HERE.
トトト—
REMI! IF YOU DON'T HURRY UP, WE'RE GOING TO LEAVE WITHOUT YOU!
BLAH. I CAN FIND MY OWN WAY, SO STOP FUSSING!
WHY YOU-!!

REBIRTH

Introduction:

It has been more than three hundred years since the powerful Sorcerer Kalutika betrayed the vampire Deshwitat, murdering his beloved Lilith and casting him into a realm of eternal darkness. Trapped between the land of the living and the land of the dead, Deshwitat has plotted his revenge. Now, at long last, his time is at hand.

In a capricious twist of fate, Deshwitat is resurrected by a modern-day team of spiritual investigators—Professor Sangho Do, his plucky daughter Remi, and the beautiful young exorcist Millenear—each one threatened by death at the hands of dark demons. In an act of noble self-sacrifice, Do offers his life to the weakened vampire in exchange for protecting the two women. And so a precarious alliance forms. In order to destroy Kalutika, Deshwitat needs Millenear to help him learn the "Power of Light." In return, the vampire agrees to aid Remi in bringing her father back from the grave.

The lines between good and evil...light and dark...morality and immorality...all begin to blur in this macabre tale of revenge and redemption. The vampire genre has been given fresh life in the pages of this new Korean import, *Rebirth*.

Created by:
Woo

Release Date:

T
TEEN
AGE 13+

PRIEST

THE QUICK & THE UNDEAD
IN ONE MACABRE MANGA.
AVAILABLE NOW

CATREECE! CATREECE! IT'S ME, COLLIN!
IT IS YOU, ISN'T IT, CATREECE?
RUSTLE...
STUB!
ALBERT MEEKS 1952 2012 LATER DUDE
MAN! THIS VIRTUAL STUFF REALLY WORKS! THAT REALLY HURT!
THUD
OUCH!
....
NOW WHERE DID SHE GO?

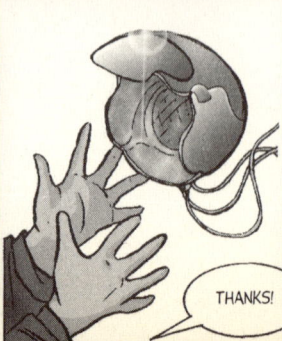

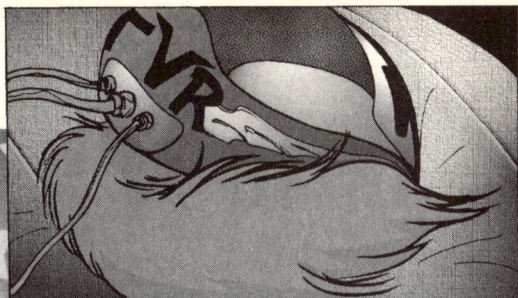

MUST...
GET...
TO...
ERK'S...